How Light Reaches Us

How Light Reaches Us

by

Kristin Berger

© 2024 Kristin Berger. All rights reserved.
2nd Edition, Kelsay Books, 2024.
1st Edition, Kelsay Books, 2016.
This material may not be reproduced in any form, published,
reprinted, recorded, performed, broadcast,
rewritten, or redistributed without
the explicit permission of Kristin Berger.
All such actions are strictly prohibited by law.

Cover design by Shay Culligan
Cover art by Rakar West. "Thunderstorm I,"
oil & wax on panel, 18" x 24"
Author photo by Kristin Berger

ISBN: 978-1-63980-660-7

Kelsay Books
502 South 1040 East, A-119
American Fork, Utah 84003
Kelsaybooks.com

Acknowledgments

Much gratitude to the editors of the journals and publications who first published many of these poems, most in different forms:

Arc Poetry Magazine: "Eddy Line"
The Blue Hour: "Desire Path"
Camas: "Blaze" (as "Sophia Answers Journey")
Cirque: "Kindling," "The Pain and Bliss of Hibernation"
Elohi Gadugi: "Moraine" (as "When the Owl Powers Over")
MiPOesias: "Scorpion Weed," "*Sonder*, in Reverse"
Orion Online: "A Thin Accumulation" (as "My Lake")
Poecology: "Aimless Drainage," "Kisstank," "Oxbow"
Untitled Country Review: "Inside-Out"
Verseweavers: "Our Own Private Alaska"
The Wayfarer Journal: "Drifting on Small Lake," "First Ice"
Writing the Land: Wanderings II: "Mosier Plateau"

"At the End of Paths Taken" is borrowed from The Cowboy Junkies' album of the same name, Latent Recordings, 2007.

"Our Own Private Alaska," a collaboration with Scot Siegel, was awarded 2nd Place Prize by the Oregon Poetry Association in Fall 2012 and appeared online at The Poetry Storehouse.

Deep thanks to Playa at Summer Lake, Oregon, for residencies in 2013 and 2015, giving me time, space, inspiration and companionship to write many of these poems. Gratitude for: Nancy Flynn, who read various drafts and gave valuable feedback; Cindy Mom, friend and reader, who gave me a copy of *HomeGround* and knew I'd have fun with it; Will Vaughan, for her longtime support, and for her photography, which inspired some of these poems; Scot Siegel, poet and partner, who contributed in countless ways to the editing and crafting of this book. And to my children, Alice and Margot, always there, under the poems.

Contents

I. Desire Path

The Scaffolding That Is Us at Night	15
Glade	16
Thunder at Dawn	17
Inside-Out	18
Eddy Line	19
Desire Path	20
Our Own Private Alaska	21
The Ninth Moon	22
Scorpion Weed	23
At the End of Paths Taken	24
Oxbow	25
The Pain and Bliss of Hibernation	26

II. This Searing Season

Kindling	29
Mere	30
Aimless Drainage	31
Spur	32
Kisstank	33
Jaral	34
Thalweg	35
Céja	36
Apron	37
Moraine	38
Pushcover	39
Badger	40
Despoblado	41
Coyote Well	42
Blaze	43

III. Subduction Zone

Passenger   47
Rock Flour   48
Rut   49
Subduction Zone   50
Fault Springs   51
Spoil Bank   52
Playa   53
Urban Viewshed   54
Mosier Plateau   55
Archipelago   56

IV. How Light Reaches Us

Summer Triangle   59
Stream Sink   60
Slack Tide   61
First Ice   62
Drifting on Small Lake   63
Talus   64
Beginning to See   65
Cresting   66
Rift Valley   67
100% Illuminated   68
The Lost Wind Locates Itself   69
A Thin Accumulation   70
Sonder, in Reverse   71

for my loves

I. Desire Path

Get close to things that slide away in the dark.

—Tom Hennen

The Scaffolding That Is Us at Night

Along a dark city block, the burnt tug of fall overtakes breath—
no warning when streetlights blaze or stop
or the sweep of an opened door spills warm music out.
Small porches sidle up to houses like goldens.
Air circles and circles as if it has lost hold of a hand
at a crossing, retracing spent kisses in the shadows.
Through a drying scrim of oak, bulbs pitch a blue-white haze.
Below, a litany of parings dance—little disco eclipses—
a thousand collaborations between night and the world.
We bend low in the grid, look up to trace the source,
before snow flies.

Glade

Lines blur. No season: all seasons matted into one.
Spring's swarm and pulse.
Winter rummaging the tosselled curve of buckthorn.
Summer divines its wayward course.
In the way she succumbs to the grass, Fall cannot help but sleep
like an abandoned dream among the cows.
Day becomes unattached to its arch.
Lapwings walk across her face as if her hair were their future nests.
A cat lay a fat rabbit at her feet. Air toggles iris blue.
The sliver of moon and the river, bending far off, are really lovers,
though they rarely find the time to lie with one another.

Thunder at Dawn

Wake in the pitch.

A train, far off, is as insistent
as a rusted tragedy.

Under generations of quilts
unknotting in the swivel

let go of warmth
and count the seconds

between kiss and tempest.

Inside-Out

I meant
I'd string myself up
to the next passing cloud
one that looks threatening
like it could do damage
could turn this moment inside-out
could reach from the ceiling of someone
else's soul and touch down in mine
that nook that hasn't seen light
in quite a few years
the place piled thick
with still-alive lichen
sperm whale teeth
rotting readable books
maps missing their legends
that gray littered place—

I'd welcome some stirring
a leveling—hold onto
the braid of the past
present and future
unraveling in the funnel
try and steer myself
to that calm center
I've heard so much about
where you can see all of it
whirling around like barn doors
and bewildered cows—
your promise ring levitating
on its revived chain
the inscription as clear as ink

when I asked you to write me back.

Eddy Line

The creek shudders
against trestle beams
a low, treble song,
and dusk dissolves light
into night's scoured pool.
A ready basket. Your kiss
would be the dark floor.
I would crawl for it
feel my way
through matted branches
towards the ripe plum
turn the globe
in my palm and buff
fog from its skin—

No need to cross the line.
I have tasted you my whole life.

Desire Path

Some days we need half-sleep
to set our raw
assumptions aside—

sheet saddling hip
a threadbare gesture

that lets the hand stray

unhinge and take, with care
each divine fold
of doubt—

dreams clear their throats

know enough to keep
to themselves like purring

things in the dark.

Our Own Private Alaska

So, this is how it's done—
camp smoke and a hard nap—

We could stay here, suckle on latitude
sickness, settle into an acute

daydream: nunataks above the noon
noise, ice-clutched flags of green

auroras. How could it be so simple?—
the sea stippled, though no wind—

and you and I so close under a patch
of sky arched and aching.

The Ninth Moon

Since peaches
were first coaxed
into jars. Half-moons
and quartered globes
fill each other, honeyed,
still blushing.

Scorpion Weed

An antiquated hum is rising, *phacelia*
pushing up into the bellies of bees,
full-throttle dance, the sun all at once—
there is no single bloom to rasp
tongue against, sink into.
We could be the honey,
the final idling after legs comb
through spent lavender curls
swallowing each soft body into their hulls.
We could hide for days, no trace,
like deer slipping into their bed,
or a king and queen chambered
against day and night believing
the field is theirs—everywhere the thrum,
bristling, like a universe of wildfires.

At the End of Paths Taken

Shadows slide over the just thawed pond
and windows brim with breath.
She sleeps on a raft of sage dreams.
The sun tats her hair with motes.
He leans his face into the nozzle
as to a lion licking all the corners he forgot,
and rinses himself, skin opalescent,
laced with musk and ocean.
Through steam, the last light finds him.
Stars replenish themselves in their marrow,
ever devoted to the margins.

Oxbow

Slip out of the main stem of the world,
oversized and rushing with its crude loads
of wheat and oil and the driven wind.

Detour. Collect storms and cottonwood crowns
cast down, a sweet freight, slow-shuttled,
true to what ballasts it against the dark
currents of an old, restless river.

Gusts of light rake our blue crescent.
They reach low, like rain's cool hands
and hold this new contour—patient
for a pulsing wake that can bear anything.

The Pain and Bliss of Hibernation

Hanging over the lid of the next storm, light is never snuffed.

What would the bear imagine if she could wake, for a moment,
from the creep of winter, peer up the hollowed tree trunk,
aurora borealis blowing through with a metallic howl—
could she sense beyond the dim heat of her body
banking around the memory of him, in her?
A new animal takes root, colorless claws digging in
and ember of heart pivoting towards her weary one.

The cold is a welcome friend.

It has taken all her strength to find night's tip-pit,
breath rippling in the portal.
As soon as they surface, dreams of meadows un-knit,
steam releasing from her pelt like river fog.
Days without her pass over, searching, and snow blots
the scent of her other children, room now
only for slow blood eddying towards spring—

The devouring of warmth, the next front,
the wasting, the giving over.

II. This Searing Season

*Because when God opened a window Something had to be done.
Walking into the landscape, the faithful are departing.
This is the far-off country I'm writing you from.*

—Eva Saulitis

Kindling

How drought begins:
two trunks too close, juniper roots
tapping the same source.

I cannot pitch a clothesline.

The air thins out like the mail.
Twelve lilac runts, burlap-balled,
teeter around our shack like tallow candles—

Seasons infiltrate
like cottonwood dander.

Bull snakes camp by the well.

I write letters, paper the walls.
Bedsprings answer with the lack of urgency.

He said he'd come back with the rains,
that sharp time of sage
blooming from skirts.

I drape linens over lilac skeletons,
a perimeter of surrender—

Nothing now but gauze,
my need to ignite
reined in.

Mere

Mother knew almost nothing of men,
only that they had to be fed.
Down from the Licking
they stood under her bare bulb,
porch boards caked with coal.
She let them in.
Dollar-fifty a night. Locked
from the inside, she slept on
the only white linen
sheets in town.

Aimless Drainage

So what if my handwriting is too fanciful for my age?
Out here, wind sneaks through a barroom door
and ranch-hands blow in, clearing tables faster
than you can swipe a wet rag before the next round—
Out here, a girl needs to write her name forwards
and backwards on the bathroom wall, filling every gulch
between picked apart flowers and hearts shot
through with arrows. She holds her own, loops
under and around talk of back roads, flatbeds and boys
that go nowhere in this valley that floods
every hundred years with love letters it scrawls to itself.

Spur

Don't most girls dream of riding bareback,
nothing between them and the moonlit distance
but owls and the bark of old dogs?
They keep their hair uncut
and twitch in their sleep.

Kisstank

In June's arms, I could have lived.
She cured those parched thoughts of boys
who held yellow-rumped warblers
stunned against windshields until
hearts slowed in their rough palms,
boys who'd trade a kiss for a life.

She knew those high, flat rocks
where women ground seed from chaff,
varnished small desert bowls cupping
rain and the resuscitated moon—
where she taught me to drink
slowly, deeply and often.

Jaral

Late into the night, we two-stepped
like lovers polishing the hardpan,
our dance tangled in barbed wire
and rockroses braiding across
the old lakebed . . .

Or were we hunting?

Soft scuffle-marks derange
from dugouts like lace ripped
loose from a skirt.

Hard to say. Dawn confuses
night's long-whipped shadows
with moonlight snagged in our hair:
proof of this strange love
loping the steppe like hunger.

Thalweg

Thighs shelter
this branched talk

the dark way
we don't touch:

divided by more
than figments—

sinew-strung pulse
rain-tamped skin

river pillowing
into the silt

of our discourse,
the embedded light.

Céja

She's not sure she should follow
my thin name and hunger
for scarp. Footsore up here
she keeps her sunglasses on.
Sun-seared pinion.
She eyes me and the slick
rock that does not promise
a good night's sleep.

Apron

When in doubt, be in plain sight
and the desert will hide
you in her skirt-folds
until coyote's teeth fade.

Moraine

When the owl powers over
and knifes the pitched night,
a January moon flutes through
Jack pine, pools on new snow.
Black River holds its breath—
center of the years iced over,
a thin accumulation.
No tracks on a hammered freeze,
this plow line, this road out.

That summer, Grandfather took
a black garbage bag, a shovel
and lemonade sweating up the jar
back into state land and had me
steal saplings, root balls and all,
a dozen slung wings over his shoulder—

Silence in the quiver.
Sand drifted through bracken and bushes.
Each stunted blueberry swallowed,
as sweet as ice, in his black wake.

Pushcover

Force me into hiding
and this is what I become:
Pelt before death, bones
beaded to nerves
keeping company of quail
who have no sense
but to call out.

I know you: the piss
on your leg, blunt barrel
at your beveled heel—
Lake of sky glints
off the stretch
of your shadow.

Sly intertwine
covet my heart
murmur and welcome
me in.

Badger

In the silent, culling fields, nothing is left to burn,
every last juniper fencepost charred to ash.
The firestorm that swept over the ridge like lava,
loose and rangy, rooted all thoughts of home
burrowed deep in the bitterbrush.
Eyes pasted shut. Blistered finger whorls.
Nest of hair, frayed and singed.
Winter, an ice sheet soon to lock bones.
To survive the coming wind-whips, I befriend
at last, that dismantling, hot-breathed animal,
that bank of fur smoldering in the scree.

Despoblado

My tongue is done lashing dunes.
The boards of my floor will never level
fit for a cradle, keep windy lullabies in tune.
When each of you was plucked
like birds shimmying south,
I dug into alkali until my blood cooled
in stacks lining desert shelves,
my belly forever soft from all it held
what it might yet come to bear—
Done drinking the scarp's black seep,
my tongue is my own pestle to grind.

Coyote Well

Sister, come quick! All is not lost—
the well has not spoiled.
Seal Mother's bucket with milk,
mix seed and sand and bone into
the baked rows, our ashed mouths
already so full of pale, musk melon.
Chink this bawling wind with rinds
flung to the agitated skyline.
Tie our aprons with blood
wiped fresh from necks. Never
again trust a man to paw
at his soured dreams. We'll outlast
this searing season, stay
two steps ahead of weather
and beast circling our sweet,
blind, bottomless hope.

Blaze

A love letter from a Wolf Mother

Overnight, the topographical map refuses
to match—washed-out green swatches
bleed unrecognizable down the range.

I am not long after you, but snared
between forks that force me north
to the Mighty River, a long lapping,

its silted brew only a memory
of land. My abandoned gait.
My mouth slick with moth fat.

The bowl of me hunts for a cool
scrabble to den down in—
I have only myself now to nuzzle.

Rank miner's caves bristle
with the rumor of cougars
on a backward breeze: I slip

beneath the fire lookout tower; the man
senses my heat, a thin cloud
with no strike, a restless

evaporation. Listen child. Hold
your magnetic nerve to cross
volcanic vertebrae and state lines.

Trespass. Make them wince
at your shadow. Spread unwelcome
seeds riding your pelt. Lodge yourself.

I will keep feasting on meat
locked in river ice,
that pale blue throat-song . . .

She is the patient echo
at the edge of your sunrise.

III. Subduction Zone

I wanted to be ready for whatever was left of the world.

—Clair Wamanholm

Passenger

This is the last you'll ever hear from us, she wrote on the back of a gas station receipt, which refused to lay flat on the kitchen counter. A full tank, the cheapest grade. *Please Come Again!* printed dutifully across the bottom. *Don't try to find us.* He did not blink but looked to the sky, the weather advancing like a flock of starlings. Drifts of future days, blowing through, leaving the trees stripped. She would take the back roads. She would roll the windows all the way down just to catch sleet in her teeth. Maps and pens and books so high the passenger seat belt alarm sounded. She could pivot towards her own extinction, if she chose. Her small, saucer-eyed daughter in the backseat. Hers, too. But a peace resembling flight takes shape in her fog lights. The white paint strip holds her away from the edge, expands into a red night full of possibilities blazing in her rear-view mirror.

Rock Flour

She always has the endgame in sight.
Hot, cold, she can stay still for epochs,
like granite, wait for wind to shift her hair
but not her mind. She wants to know
what's coming for her, what drama
will be deposited at her feet next—
A friend's cancer. A parent's memory loss.
Childhood becoming a rare nunatak
where black wings of Magdalena alpine bask
until sun overtakes. The anger she no longer needs
to shed like terminal dust at the edge of a grudge.
What trauma she would release like blue ribbons
of meltwater down the currents of memory,
if she could only let go of the story she's been telling
herself for thousands of suns—her sadness
could retreat, exposing joy, a fine white silt
dusting her long, empty arms.

Rut

She got out just in time, before night cleaved day away
from the bone. An arctic freeze swallowed the hills.
The burn at flood stage and rising from the week's rain,
the crossroad washed out. She found another way.
The little chapel in the village rang its old iron clapper
like a bell at sea. Someone would have polished the pews'
arm rests into a mahogany sheen. Not many would brave
the evening down the ice-pitched lanes, only the determined,
the thick-coated souls. She made it just before the doors
were double bolted, propped up her mud-clotted boots
on the kneelers and looked up. A weak sun setting in the apse,
each chip of glass stained red, green, ancient yellow and milk blue.
A sun ready to receive and hold until the last note of the organ
floated up to where all prayers congregated. Up there where time
was not locked. Where God sometimes answered with thaw
and warmth, a catching of breath, and the light spilling over.

Subduction Zone

The lake is sinking and there's nothing anybody can do about it.
Each night, I wait for the moon to come back, shine near.
There will be fewer stars because of the floodlight,
but I want to be filled. I offer a map of unreachable caves
to a friend whose heart is stranded on an ancient lakebed
of grief but have no legend or key or idea of distance.

Thousands of years after the lake reached its high watermark—
when the first people tuned their minds to small waves lapping,
water still finds the right places to lie. Lovers find their way, too,
after years of estrangement. Their beds dot the playa,
rabbitbrush whorls and dust devil depressions, ready to receive.

Once, I found the wind-brushed body of a coyote, maybe asleep,
or curled for nursing. She let go of the idea of the lake as easily
as life. She sank, and I, with my breathing, uncurled body, rose,
and ran away.

Fault Springs

Snow fell the second I stepped out of the hot springs—
he tells his wife on a Friday night—changed from corn
to fat on the drive back. It's good to see snow, again,
even though it will melt tomorrow. 70 degrees by noon.
The cup really is half-full—he says into the wind—
sometimes with mineral water, sometimes with light.

Spoil Bank

Choking on scotch broom's blackened
pods splayed in the till, we cling
to a scuff-mark's hill-of-beans-hope
that rain will come, our banks will spill
and we will be resuscitated.
Tell me that the seed cleaved
to a tire's branded tread is no less
than the burnished tomato tripping
into an heirloom willow basket—
we strive to ripen in places
no one expects.

Playa

You say we are standing at the edge of the past—
undrainable, violent in its captive seasons,
layers, records, what's worth remembering.
What we latch onto when scanning the horizon
in the white heat. What works its way stranded
to the surface, your snapshots of love, friends
not yet dead, alkali pain you keep like pearls
under-tongue. I say, the edge is all we have—
the future blooms over us, a clean sweep
of sun and moon, their exquisite arching,
the next day, into night, smoothing our regret.
Stars forget to be a body when falling,
extinguishing themselves in showers.
Under this present blue agreement
between crust and sky, inland oceans
will make a small deposit on our shore.

Urban Viewshed

The houseless man washes his upper body
in plain sight next to a six-lane freeway bisecting
a neighborhood's heart, all four chambers hard
at work remaining viable, and strong.
Cropped butterfly bushes tremble under
barbed wire hemming a wrecking yard—
cottonwood sheds its simple weight, drifting up
and over his prime sleeping places like a dune.
Trained to skirt the years, he knows the blur
of green brush hides more than just coyote scat,
welcomes him as if this moment is a reverie,
as if his life was not on display
for everyone to ignore.

Mosier Plateau

—for the Friends of the Columbia Gorge

Climb over rocks and ruts, skirt crimson poison oak,
yarrow stalks and California poppies clustered
like road signs on a blind curve—

Up to the first plateau where there is no wind—
balsamroot husks hold their parched golden song
of spring's riotous petal loads.

Past the pioneer cemetery set like a lawn ready
for trick-or-treaters. Weather-smoothed names,
those who died young with a lilac to guard.

There is beauty in escarpment, earth falling away
emerging across the river, the basalt slide-fault
like a loaf of bread ripped by hungry hands . . .

Beauty in plateaus that never stop the climb,
but pause and rise and pause . . . Breathing points.
The sun etches the backs of salmon quickening

the river's pulse with silver, with emerald and ruby.
We are in the middle of a storybook ending
that never comes—white oaks remind us

that more fruit falls to the ground than is gathered.
We don't need to carry so much. Never to worry
about ever reaching the top.

Archipelago

Only one small bird comes near,
this far north, inland sea of concrete
and plywood. Anna's hummingbird dips
its needle beak into near-frozen sugar water,
her throat of fire challenging the gray dawn.
Her nest is a thought only she carries through rain.
Other residents set out feeders like lanterns, hoping
for her swift spark to hover, sip, and maybe land.
Geese also fly over, every morning, which helps
the belief in flight, in arrowing for something,
even if it's only for the same parking lot marsh.
They call to one another as if it's all brand new.
I can get behind that. I can live between
breast and wing where the heart pumps as quiet
as lovers breathe in the dark.
I would brave the seam of separation
between earth and atmosphere, a miracle
of blues, with your hand in mine. Create lift
from the body's need to let go—earth below,
spring mud beginning to swamp the air,
some faces still moved enough to look up—
I would pack my lightest shoes. I could go without.
I would lift into a life of days studding our future
like velvet green havens. I could go slowly,
strongly, sipping every minute, island to island.
I would wear love's blaze at my throat.

IV. How Light Reaches Us

The other world is also this one.

—Tomas Tranströmer

Summer Triangle

They were only boys exploring the French countryside—
a dog, a rope, a tunnel updrafting into day like a lost river.
Sweep of oil lantern light and the walls of Lascaux
rippled with bull muscle, cranes and constellations,
the undersides of time's standing wave—

In the dark, fixed by palms against limestone,
stars lived a quiet second life.

And now, just under the skin of the river,
currents hold the world's braids in a hyporheic wash.
A salmon fans her redd with a tender urgency
while her lover waits in shadows, between cairns,
white-bellied and spent, ready to give over
like the moon on its way to perigee.

Tell me, Lone Wanderer—
Does your home country taste of hope?
Do you have enough starlight to travel by?
One season to the next, can you stumble, gladly,
with no map?

Stream Sink

We drove for miles, no beginning
or end to the road through Trevelez,
phone lines slack with their loads of sun
like tortuous banks cradling a river.

At the flea market below Peñabon, in the rush
of dust and tables and tents, I lost you—
the chaos swallowed you whole.
Everywhere, goat bells cried out.

And then, like drinking from a deep well,
we found each other, clearly,
in an old mirror—upright and shabby,
but holding its tarnished charge of sky—

Faint braids of water reemerged
from the red *cascapeñas,* a stonefield
trickling with the distant song of how faithful
headwaters are to their patient, azul seas.

Slack Tide

If it takes a day, a year, an epoch of solstices
stacked like tide-upon-tide's ship-shod pages

to come to the edge of this sumptuous home,
a zenith above and beneath, then I will swallow

this full wash of light and burrow into you, angle
of no repose, no shadow, only ebb, swamped

in answer and reply, our un-mappable shore,
wade into the ever-wanting lip-upon-lip

towards the sun stalled at its grace-point,
never succumbing to the ever-cresting sea.

First Ice

When you said the possibilities were endless,
I believed every wrought-iron shape
they took under winter's heaving stonework

luring me with sleeves of openness.
Don't seal off. Ice is only light trapped
in the breath of our lived-through days

cupped in quiet curtains, beneath the weight
of incoming darkness. Forging dreams drift
like a loon's sooty call unmoored

from a remote lake—and desire slips
through the star-rimmed throat like a blaze.

Drifting on Small Lake

In the half-light, that early season when all lesser birds juggle lust
and song with fishing line and spider webs tucked into their beaks,
an osprey rushes low, dips her talons, cuts the emerald skin—
a rainbow trout rises like a promise into air's bright clutch.

I shunt the canoe into a slip of shade, a roof of blackberry blossoms,
and stroke water so heady with pollen its green pelt steeps
like a tonic silting down the lake's dark shelves, a reservoir of bones.
She loses her grip and the fish freefalls, re-enters its old, hungry life.

We are not alone in the treading. The door is left ajar and spring
sifts in; winter's bitter milk tempered out, so far from shore.

Talus

The plain, smoothed hours
nestle and tuck wind

little envelopes of days
shouldering a baking heat

anticline of any hope
for true winter

cairn to scree
bush to berry

you want to spill
into a story of lushness

a recognizable meadow
all the mountains rim

the one wide and waiting
in sweet ambush.

Beginning to See

The kitchen hums
with steam from pots
ready to boil

the odd dance
between laundered days
under an antique sconce

the hope we polish
when we remember
old patterns, the beauty

always a shard
billowing above us.

Cresting

Deep in spate, rivers of day and night
lattice the house, rain never-ending.
Streetlights hover or blink off at the first creep
of dark or light. Time smoothes the silk bedspread
while tea steeps and the car engine ticks
in the driveway, and no one embraces the fold
of pillows cold all day for some body's warmth.
But before the creek crests and flows into traffic,
while children are still young enough to sprawl across
laps and the whole world tips into a far-gone forever—
stardust avalanches off the closest mountain.
The lover's scent is an animal tracked into waking,
not yet threaded into memory's white-out—
Go to the sink for one more glass of water.
Hold it against the available light, the hot cheek,
drink it down like rain and have no fear
of running dry. Any flickering second.
While water rises to cleave the gray.

Rift Valley

No, my dear, I don't remember the rift,
only being flush with each other—
I still feel like an unbroken prairie,
limber as grass in the hard wind.
Our worn valley holds close
a little pond of ducks and willows.

Look, Love, here comes that everlasting sun
to spread its hot sheet on your depression.

Wait—let me clip your gray curls back
with the crescent moon. That's better.
See? We are still beautiful.
Let's release our faults to the stars.
Let's retire here, until time erodes us
to our great-great grandchildren's knees.

100% Illuminated

When the sun strokes your window with its *ever-striving*
and tips behind waxy laurels collecting dust,
roses climb the wall like a search party . . .

When light within balances dusk hovering over the patio
and figs coming into their fullness swarm the air,
you begin to call birds by name . . .

When panes frame every misplaced, thinned fragment—
blue water glide, midnight ice, child's hands on your chin—
breath-fog becomes summer's only cloud . . .

How light reaches us, we will never know.
Nightjars steer clear of weathervanes, make for the sea
of open sky with the rumor of how whole you really are.

The Lost Wind Locates Itself

Caught in the throat of an off-course dove.
On the lip of the Divide.
After a storm surge and before the next.
Combing clouds through cedar boughs.
When horse chestnuts thrash their candles.
Between words, spoken or silent.
Between tongues and a kiss.
Under the suspension bridge's leap-off point.
Shuttling salmon through river rock.
Between lightning and old growth.
In the joke diffusing in a bonfire.
Rimming the edge of a cave.
Within itself, within doubt.
Between fruit and the orchard floor.
In uncontained fog.
At the nape's loose lock.
Breath by breath, first to last.
In now's sweet dervish.

A Thin Accumulation

One year, my lake will have no ice. Snow will not drift, bury cabins, become an animal itself—one that everyone fears, secretly, openly, but also craves, like a lover. We want it to blanket, lull and daze. We want it to seal the fish in tight, a polar aquarium we auger into, then wait hours for their phosphorescence to reach us. All those long winter days of sitting inside, tinkering with a fire, peeling orange after orange. Then, a bluebird day. Windows let in so much reflected light we must blink it away by bringing tea-steam in close.

Birch live this whiteness, carry it all summer like candles striking here and there above the bracken. They hold vigil and bend when wind finally whips water into a chevron of whitecaps. The lake grows restless with reflection and persistent lily-pads, wants to impart some sort of future story . . . that the docks will be hauled out along with the rowboats by still-strong old men. That smokehouses will fume with fish stock-piled and salted. That it will give its surface over like a mirror for a stray comet to blur upon.

Next year, we might lay our sunburned shoulders against sheets ravining with sand and turn to each other again. All this light between skin: the shedding of and the coming new. Geese blaze the way, showing us all how to bow down low, circle open water, return and return. Crave a deep cold sleep.

Sonder, in Reverse

In the dream of the train, we sit with our backs to the engine
pulling us away from the gate, curbs, our city's bridges.
We eavesdrop on reckless conversations between river and bank,
our hands together as we head deeper into the unlit pocket—
you let go to point out an eagle high in cottonwoods
before a basalt tunnel overtakes us—silence rides the rails
like a ridge of breath, or a kiss filling each other's mouths.
I hold your face away from the light.
A bay full of geese emerges, a canvas of dark stars.
Someone waves from a brush pile, burning
winter's evidence, those rookeries of words
at home in the greening margins. The world pauses
to let us pass through. Doors slide apart and we step
onto the bright platform of our brief universe . . .

And isn't that how most dreams are constructed?
Feathers, smoke, salt and palm—
the past we rush towards, the silt-loaded river,
the swing-bridge waiting for us in the dark.

Notes

Home Ground: Language for an American Landscape (Trinity University Press, 2006), edited by Barry Lopez and Debra Gwartney, inspired the landscape-term poems. Many of the terms are colloquial, or out of use, becoming as antiquated and as diminished as the landscape, and our relationship with it, changes. An abbreviated, interpreted glossary can be read in tandem:

Aimless Drainage. Stream or river that wanders, meanders, seemingly aimlessly. A "deranged drainage" resembles large, loopy script written on the land.

Apron. Alluvial fans of a bajada, steeply sloping into a desert valley suggest the flaring pleats of a starched apron. A seemingly idle landscape, each swale holds flash flood debris and pathways for animals.

Archipelago. Both a body of sea that contains multiple islands and the islands themselves, and typically have diverse floral and faunal activity and complex, sometimes unusual, biological interfacings.

Blaze. Native Americans scored tree bark lightly with tomahawks when pursing wounded prey, to code the way back. To mark a trail is to blaze into the future by way of the past.

Céja. Literally, an "eyebrow." Figuratively: a line of trees at the edge of a meadow; a scarp; a thin strip of clouds above a chain of mountains; a sliver of moon; a narrow path.

Coyote Well. A spoiled well. Coyotes are often blamed for many poisoned, false or misleading things, but they are also renowned for their ability to find water—a true water witch.

Desire Path. A route found through habit, a shortcut to a desired place.

Despoblado. A depopulated, abandoned, sacked and feral landscape.

Eddy Line. The seam between a river's faster and slower currents. Crossing the eddy line means leaving the mainstream.

Jaral. Scrubplains, chaparral. A tangled, confused situation.

Kisstank. A pool of rainwater in a rock basin, where parched desert travelers and creatures drink eagerly and *with passion*.

Mere. Lake, pond, marsh or fen, sea, or inlet. A boundary. A siren, a mermaid. A mother.

Pushcover. Thick brush into which an animal, in a hunt, is pursued.

Rift Valley. A trough between parallel faults, caused by either the Earth's crust stretching apart or compressing together.

Rock Flour. Fine rock powder, mostly quartz, created when a glacier scrapes its way across a valley floor. It can be found threading glacial rivers like blue milk or carried great distances by the wind.

Spoil Bank. A mound of earth beside a mining tunnel, road cut, quarry, or the material dredged from canals or harbors. Plant life colonizing a spoil bank parallels the recovery of life following a receding glacier, landslide, or other catastrophe—like a seed bank.

Spur. A finger of elevated land that juts out from a mountain or ridge into lower ground but doesn't outdo its parent mountain or ridge in size. A spur trailing out to an open plain function as a funnel for animals looking to stay covered as long as possible.

Stream Sink. A creek lost to a swallow hole, which reemerges many miles away—a *tajos de chorrilo*—as a new river re-named, re-plaiting itself.

Thalweg. A stream's subterranean divide.

Viewshed. A viewshed designates a field of vision witnessed by onlookers—a forest, an ocean, anything with a reason to be scrutinized. It can also hide what its creator doesn't want it to see: clear cuts or homeless encampments, for instance.

p. 41. "Blaze" was inspired by Scot Siegel's poem "Epistles to the Imnaha Pack: Dispatches from Journey" from *The Constellation of Extinct Stars and Other Poems,* Salmon Poetry, 2016.

p. 57. "Summer Triangle" In 1940, cave paintings were discovered in Lascaux, France, by four French teenagers and their dog, Robot. They stumbled upon the caves while they were out exploring one day. The main cave is approximately 66 feet wide and 16 feet high and is connected to a number of smaller chambers. Scientists used carbon dating to estimate the age of some charcoal found in the caves, at 17,000 years old. There are about 2,000 drawings and engravings, mostly of animals: horses, bison, red deer, stags, cats, and aurochs—large, black cattle-like animals that are now extinct. There are also human figures, various geometric shapes; the outlines of human hands—possibly the signatures of the artist; and an Ice Age star chart—clusters of stars that resemble known constellations like Taurus the Bull, the Summer Triangle, and the Pleiades.

p. 69. "*Sonder*, in Reverse" takes its title from *The Dictionary of Obscure Sorrows* definition of *Sonder:*

"The realization that each random passerby is living a life as vivid and complex as your own—populated with their own ambitions, friends, routines, worries and inherited craziness—an epic story that continues invisibly around you like an anthill sprawling deep underground, with elaborate passageways to thousands of other lives that you'll never know existed, in which you might appear only once, as an extra sipping coffee in the background, as a blur of traffic passing on the highway, as a lighted window at dusk."

About the Author

Kristin Berger was born in Detroit, Michigan and raised in the surrounding suburbs and Northern Michigan. She received her BA in Creative Writing from Western Michigan University and has lived in the Pacific Northwest since 1994.

Kristin is the author of six poetry collections including *For the Willing* (2nd edition, Nightjar Poetry Press, 2024), *Earthwork* (The Poetry Box, 2022), *Changing Woman, Changing Man* (Nightjar Poetry Press, 2022), *Refugia* (Persian Pony Press, 2019), and *Echolocation* (Cirque Press, 2018).

Kristin is the recipient of residencies from Playa, OSU's Spring Creek Project and is a contributor to the Writing the Land Project, which pairs poets with nature preserves and wilderness areas. Kristin serves on the board of directors of Playa at Summer Lake and lives in Oregon.

More at:
kristinbergerpoet.com

www.ingramcontent.com/pod-product-compliance
Lightning Source LLC
Chambersburg PA
CBHW030912170426

43193CB00009BA/823